KY

Pomegranate

poems by Pomegranate
women's writing group

D1313261

Published by Stramullion Publishing and Pomegranate

ISBN 0 907343 112

A CIP catalogue record for this title is availiable from the British Library.

Acknowledgements

Some of the poems included in this anthology have been published previously, and acknowledgments are made to the following publications where the poems first appeared.

Elizabeth Burns - 'Mother and Child in the Botanic Gardens' in *Original Prints 3* (Polygon 1989); Susan Streeter Carpenter - 'Buses' in *Flights*; Maggie Christie - 'Sweet sound, sea sound, music sound' in *Original Prints 4* (Polygon 1992); Margaret Elphinstone - 'Lilies', 'Fifteen Glass Fishing Floats', 'Stealing', 'Mother' and 'Potato Cuts' in *Outside Eden* (Sundial Press 1990); Thelma Good - 'The inland train journey' in The School of Poets Calendar (1991); Mary McCann - 'Working for Moloch', 'On Craiglockhart Hill' and 'Sky' in the *Edinburgh Women's Liberation Newsletter*; Ruth McIlroy - 'Bus-stops' and 'The Coffin Lift' in *Slow Dancer*, 'Annunciation' in *Iron*, 'Plenty' in *Poetry Nottingham*, 'Interloper' in *Rialto*, 'Acid' in *North*; Susan Maťašovská - 'What lesbians do in Jenners' in *The Crazy Jig* (Polygon 1992); Maureen Sangster - 'Aberdeen' in *Northlight*, 'Scattering Ashes' in *Different People* (Straightline 1987), 'Woman' in *Chapman*, 'Unpalatable' in *Sempervivum*; Rebecca Wilson - 'For Consuella' in *Graffiti*, 'Turning Point' in *Scrievans*.

Cover illustration by Jennie House

Typeset by The Graphics Company, Edinburgh
Printed by Meigle Printers Ltd, Galashiels

The publishers would like to thank Edinburgh District Arts Council for a grant towards the publication of this book.

Contents

 ELIZABETH BURNS

Mother and child
in the Botanic Gardens
'Baby carriages are not allowed in the plant houses'

The baby floats carriage-less
in her water-lily cradle
It wafts and drifts her round the world

Australasia   Guatemala   Mexico
South Laos   Norfolk Islands   Crete

Wrapped in a coir of coconut
she floats from island to island
A bush with waxy orange flowers
bends between her and the sun
Purple berries fall into her lap
She eats them, lays her head
on the creamy pillow of a lily flower
She is lost in Tropics of the Old World
Her dreams are scented

The mother comes running through the plant houses
tropical to temperate and back to tropical
frantic between the arms of palm trees
and the tangle of passion flowers
that curl their tendrils into her hair
Fronds of fern tickle and grip
Green surrounds her, a mouth of green is
eating her with jade lips
and a moist and mossy tongue
that licks her with a limey tongue

Cacti crawl at her feet
leer from their gravel and sand
claw their spikes and prickles into her skirts
The iron skeleton buckles and caves
Its bony fingers waver in the lily pond

She looks into the ochre water
and sees, curled on the deck
of a waterlily leaf, her daughter –
her eyes gazing up at the glass roof
and her mouth stained with purple

The last day of February, 1991

Mull all week has been drizzly
blotched skies blurring the view
across the water to Iona

That day you wake to sunlight
on each petal of the white hyacinth
the sea freshly blue

You turn on the radio: they say
the war is over
You stand in your nightdress, listening

Later, after a shower that washes away
so much
you put on music

and the whole room is filled with it
and with a new clear light
In the window, a different landscape

You go out into sweet air
touch the just-opened crocus
its pale petals purple-veined

walk over the hill to the harbour
take a ferry across the sound
you have looked out upon all week

Iona in its tenderness
is a new-born, baby island
tasting, for the first time, spring

In a beach garden, light fills
green glass fishing floats
There's a circle of snowdrops

Above cloisters carved with lilies
doves rest on a bell tower,
white wings against a blue sky

In the abbey there are candles
'To be lit for peace in the Gulf'
You light one, for thanksgiving

a tiny flame, hardly visible
in the bright arched window
with the sea behind

A lemon-scented geranium
patterns stone with leaf-shadows
Light falls on an old worn carpet

You take the year's first picnic
on a beach of pale sand
Green sea licking the rocks

The juice of an apple on your fingers
washed off in salt-water
dabblings for shells

On the boat going home
you glimpse a rainbow
spun across the sea

linking the two islands
in a span of frail
and watered light

as, the next morning, before dawn
the full apricot moon
will lay a path of light

across dark water
from the abbey to the bay
that laps your garden

Damson jam

In a break from work, we drink tea, and eat oatcakes
spread with your Aunt Hester's damson jam
that is sweet and tart and drips off the flat
oatcakes onto our lickable fingers.
She's a wonderful jam-maker, you tell me
has a whole larder full of jars
spends her summers and autumns making preserves.
We finish eating, get back to our work
with the taste of damsons on our mouths.

The table is spread with books and papers –
I'm writing, you're reading feminist theory,
about women being forced into roles, you say,
having to make a culture out of what they're given
– then subverting it, being good at it, making it their own.
'Like Aunt Hester's damson jam?' 'Exactly.'

Your teenage daughter comes in, pours herself tea,
asks what you're working on. You tell her.
'Oh yes,' she says, familiar, and I think:
To have a mother who does such things,
to have a daughter who accepts them,
who knows that reading books on women writers
is as natural a thing for a mother to do
as making jam.
          Then she, seventeen, who has feminism
in her blood, who knew with her milk-teeth
what it took us years to learn
goes back to her room, to her sewing.

And I think of the hours of my adolescence
given over to learning to sew, how I hated it,
how the gimlet eyes of my mother were always
checking tacks, darts, hems, neatness.
Dressmaking was my mother's art: nothing in it
too difficult for her. It didn't send her into rages
but came easily, enjoyably, as to your daughter.
I struggled clumsily, thinking that this was what
I ought to do, that it would, as was impressed upon me,
be useful and necessary. Writing, book-learning –
these were the secret, underground pleasures
not praised and admired like a home-made frock.

Katy comes in again for needles.
You glance up over glasses from your book.
I carry on writing my poem.
The jar of damson jam gleams on the table.

Dragons in the carpark

Break up the tarmac
of a carpark in Quebec
and you'll find Chinatown

You'll find the carcass
of an old laundry
the skull of the laundryman
still bound with a blue rag

You'll find his iron, rusted
and a birdcage with a scrap
of songbird left inside
You'll find an ink-brush, hardened
disintegrating paper
a sliver of calligraphy
You'll find shards of glass
and mah-jong tiles of ivory

Dig and you'll forget the rotten, fetid stink
remember instead fresh fish, lemon juice
the perfume of roses, smoky tea

Dig and you'll find the teeth of old men
fallen from soft gums
A pool of wax-melt, unstrung beads
umbrella spikes and crumbled leather shoes
A shabby suitcase lying open like a mouth

Dig and you'll find the scales of dragons
Dig and you'll remember festivals of fire
How you danced and sang then
How dragons pranced in the streets
swishing their tails of scarlet, orange, green
and flew, it seemed, with gorgeous wings

And how you set your paper lanterns on the river
dreamt they'd sail as far as ice floes
but saw the candles falter and the lanterns drown
beneath the weight of soaked paper

Dig and you'll let the dragons out again
out into the trampled carpark
See them take the tin cars in their mouths
and spit them out on bulldozed land

See, as your fingers trawl for memories
for scraps of bone or gold
see, as the sidewalk cracks apart
the dragons of your childhood rising, breathing fire

At the window

(from a painting by Chagall)

See the golden crescent of the moon
a lantern in the twilight blue
and beyond, the shadow
of another, darker, bluer
midnight moon

See in the lantern moon glow
a wee fir tree
brushed with frost

See the snow-cloud
white as washing

See it drift over the green field
where it's already spring
and the trees are frothy with blossom
and the farmers rest in the sun

See around the window
on the room's green walls
the patterning of faint, white
shapes of flowers
lily-of-the-valley maybe
their bell clusters
their heart-shaped leaves
and that perfume
in the cold green room

See above the window frame
caught between blue sky and green walls
the pale figure of a man
hovering over the room
reaching out to pluck the bunches
of white lily flowers

See the woman in the warm red blouse
rising from her green chair
with its wicker seat
to stroke the cat
who crouches on the windowsill
ready to leap
into the frosty, woodsmoke night
into the green fields, into the snow

See the angel-man touch
the curved red back of the woman
with fingertips as light
as lily-perfume

See the woman, smiling
climb onto the back of the cat

See them leap out of the window
into snow fields, into green fields
into blue sky, into thick cloud

See the sprinkling of frost
the scattering of blossom petals

See them flying
through winter and spring
see them flying
up into the space
between two moons

SUSAN STREETER CARPENTER

Fragment from the Parthenon

A horse's nose
is the softest thing –
it touches but an instant,
a warm breath,
and the horse moves off,
is gone.

Stroke a young man's neck,
wisps of hair
behind the ear –
it's sheer delight and,
in all the strains
and heaves of youth,
quickly forgotten.

But
the Athenian sculptor
remembered. In a headlong rush
of athletes riding, in
dust and sweat and heat
he caught the horse,
in marble,
whuffling gently forever
the boy's sweet ear.

Buses

They're almost always leaving,
pulling from the stop
just as you come running up,
knees aching, lungs heaving.

That bus will be a friend
who wears your number on its face.
It vows to take you to a place
of rest, safe harbour, journey's end.

With wheezes, puffs and gasps, it slows,
noses to your stop and opens wide:
"Get on, it's warm inside!"
It closes, jolts and groans, and goes.

Buses travel slowly, shove,
jerk, push and pull us; we
must struggle for our dignity:
"So sorry." "T's allright, Love."

Buses keep you in suspense.
At times, in certain phases of the moon
your faithful Five may switch its route.
The driver of course has the reason:
"We always change our course this season.
I'm turning here, you'd best get out.
There'll be a Fifteen coming soon
which you can ride for thirty pence."

A bus stop is a lonely place.
You stare down the horizon, waiting
for the bus whose promises are true.
It surfaces, comes looming into view
but hold your eagerness, abating,
until you know the number on its face.

Salmon run

Through rain, fern, fir-wood
forest, mud trail, we come
to watch the salmon.
By the boiling burn, brown brothy,
icy cold, we lean – oh, there!
One jumps,
straight up and over
the stone which rears
mid-creek – then another
heaves herself and falls
back down and away, her
dark body packed with soft roe,
to fight again
the rocks, the torrent.

The whole world runs
against the salmon, doomed
to rise above it
again, again and again.
Some leap light as dragonflies.
Some are heavy as old boots.
Some spawn, successful,
in quiet mountain pools others
have died trying to reach, not knowing
that we saw the impossible
done, the struggle
made flesh.

The vamp makes bread

So I've done with necks.
Those dives for the jugular
leave me cold. I've come in
from the prowl, okay

except for the hollow
honed hunger in my lantern
hips, charged magnet hands,
hot salt mouth.

Oh, need –
to slit open, sink
to the root of the gorge,
touch bone.

Oh, the sweet blue
veins inside his arm, mixed
with taste of fingernails, warm
dark, and smoke from a
hillside in the evening.

With yeast and milk, my
naked hands knead
the lump of lust, soothe it
limpid as earlobes, strong
as gristle, tight as rope.

Now shape a loaf, coil it,
ready to sweat and swell,
to hiss fermented woes
into the dark oven, to come
out breathing scented light.

So I'm healing, whole
and home; the fire nests
in the hearth. Children sit
round the table, gaping questions.
This bread will fill their mouths.

MAGGIE CHRISTIE

Stone Circle One

First light
reveals
the stone circle of your face

We share
the cup
of stone and water

We grow
as fast
as plants
drumming

blackness

inside the grass, the hill
considers
blackness

inside the bark, the tree
considers
blackness

out of blackness, the tree
gives birth
to greenness

inside the grass, the hill
embraces
blackness

inside the sun, whiteness
is
unbearable

inside the earth
blackness
embraces
life.

And the bands played on

(going to concerts jan/feb 1991)

On the eve of day zero
Messiaen's *Quartet for the end of time*
The work of a youngster imprisoned in time of war
The piano crashes, symbol of nothing
The violin a sea of glass
The mystic's sign of eternity

Day twenty-three, but we cease to count
As days become weeks and our lives go on
And Janáček, grown old in an unfree country
Shatters our war with hair-raising fanfares of peace and justice
Seven trumpets, and seven again
And they return over and over in triumph.
Yet this piece was once called military.

After the end, we glide home on ice.
After the end, the desert burns.

Sweet sound, sea sound, music sound

Sweet sound, sea sound, music sound, silence,
Sweet sea, sound sound, sound music, stop.
Sound sea, sound music, sweet sound, silence,
Sweet silence, sweet music, silent sea, sadness

The thought of you startles me like a poppy
An explosion of blood-red light

Sweet sweet sound, understanding of music,
Sympathy, carefulness, caring, sweetness.

Invisibility. Behind the breath control
The speech control. Support is necessary
To make the sound. Then real playing
Can begin. Unsupported breath
Makes expressionless noise, signifying nothing.

Unsupported love in my thoughts
And all around me too unseen.

Supported love is on display
The black cloud carries the sun away
Over the threshold to the wedding day.

Sweet sound, sea sound, music sound, silence,
Sweet sea, sound sound, sound music, stop.
Sound sea, sound music, sweet sound, silence,
Sweet silence, sweet music, silent sea, sadness

You are a disruptive passage in a minor key
With jerky unanswered rhythms
The thematic connection revealed
Only on repeated hearings

Sadness. Sea. Silence. Music. Sweetness.

normality/refrain

a woman is screaming
a man is being normal
a woman is screaming and screaming
a man is being normal
refrain
a man is being normal

a woman is working to death
a man is being normal
a woman is beaten to death
a man is being normal
a woman is raped to death
a man is being normal
refrain
a man is being normal

a girl is being abused
a man is being normal
a woman is powerless to help her
a man is being normal
refrain
a man is being normal

men have to change
just stop being normal
men just have to change
stop being normal
refrain
just stop being normal
just refrain
stop being normal

Garden House

The garden is full of rain,
And nothing is growing but rain.
The house is full of garden,
And nothing is held out of the house.
The side of the house dissolves,
There is nowhere in the house without storm.
The lament overpowers the duplicator
And nothing is propagated but screams.
The rain grows longer and fatter,
Seeds ripen into hailstones,
Nothing is growing but anger.
The raped woman regains her self.

The Stair Card

It is your turn to sweep and wash the common man this week.

Next week, after you've done it,
You may pass the duty to the next woman.

Many steps make a revolution.

This one has no title.

I decide to eat the orange.
Someone has cut the top off.
I peel it roundly with a knife.
Why is it so easy?

Inside, it is unnaturally pale,
Like a grapefruit.
I taste it – it is not sweet.
The orange is a lemon.

 MARGARET ELPHINSTONE

Thinking of you, in Gandolfi's

Blue fishes swim
Against a sea of rain
Above lamplight, mirrored
In grey, glorious day.
I have a private life
That's yours: two selves reflected
In naked colour
On a grey city.

Now, at a café table,
I sit still, polite,
While lit reflections
Flame within –
You – electric
Under my skin.
I eat bread decorously,
Clothed in the public eye,
So no one knows.

Lilies

Instead of buying a pint of milk
I got lilies:
Six flame-red, six sun-yellow;
A third of the family allowance
Burning like Blake's heaven
In the heart of the sitting room.
I drink tea, and read reviews
While they consume me. I remember
The rest of my life
Is my own, all mine.
Flowers meet my sideways glance
With acquiescent fire,
A conflagration
On my green tablecloth
Among the biscuit crumbs.

Fifteen Glass Fishing Floats

Eight pink ones
Were under a rock on Colonsay
The day we walked to Balnahard
To test your birthday telescope.
We split them;
I kept four.

The pale green one from Nibon
Gleamed in the tide's debris
When we crossed over
In Jane's rubber boat
And made a fire of driftwood on the beach.

Seven were scattered like magpies
Along a windswept mile of sand
South of Rosslare –
I was in love then,
Walking up and down
While the waves dazed me –

Two at Noness,
One still in its net;
The children were intent,
Fishing in rockpools.

One waited in the window
Of the house with the cherry tree
The day we moved in.

I have kept fifteen fishing floats
Out of the tide's reach.
Sometimes I dust them, in a fit
Of unaccustomed housekeeping.

I sold six at an auction
When I was broke
And wasn't sure what mattered.

On wakeful nights
I regret their loss
Among other things.

Stealing

Going with Jenny to the goats
Up the track through the wood,
We fetch water, the dogs and I,
Breathing goat smells on the wet hill.
Each goat comes up to feed,
Letting her milk down
Through my friend's hands;
The pail fills cleanly white.
Then we let the chickens out.
In winter there are horses to be fed.

Stealing the rhythm
Of someone else's day
Around the seasons slowly changing,
Weather turning our mornings
Softly or cruelly
To our varying ways.

Now I go with Janet
To her studio, up two flights
Of tiled stone steps.
The building reeks of paint.
She pins her work, unfinished, to the wall:
Landscape transmuted
Into raw perception;
I want to get my hands dirty too.

Stealing the flash
Of someone else's pain,
The city changes like lightning.
I walk home, and see
Geraniums in a grey yard,
Furious, volcanic red.

Before Paolo Uccello's
Saint George and the Dragon

One soul between us both, dragon and I,
Tethered by a thread, to each other bound;
When I am rescued, my dragon must die.

Cave in the mountain, vortex in the sky,
Seeking oasis, my self is all I found,
One soul between us both, dragon and I.

No words between us, no language to lie,
Eyes for my mirror now, fire all around;
When I am rescued, my dragon must die.

Song from the forest echoing my cry,
Dragon flames and leaps, thunders back the sound,
One soul between us both, dragon and I.

Flying the wild zone, gloriously high,
Deserts of solitude coldly surround;
When I am rescued, my dragon must die.

A dragon betrayed will never ask why;
Dying eyes cloud over, blood upon the ground.
One soul between us both, dragon and I,
When I am rescued, my dragon must die.

Mother

The innocent are so thoughtless.
They quite fail to reckon
who carries the burden of their years.
I have held emotion out of your reach,
and household bills,
and printed letters in brown envelopes.
I have dealt with all these matters
that you never thought of. The cat that squeaks
at the back door for breakfast
before I can fill the kettle, these children
who think the sun will rise and set
as long as food appears on tables,
and that clothes will be washed
as rhythmically as water following the moon
and that this house is alive and loving,
pulsing with nurture, its heating coming on
as inevitably as the first frost in September,
and the windows cleaning themselves in springtime
before the swallows.

I am tired of holding these delusions
in hands that are so far innocent,
having not yet built the monument
which will make everything different –
the whole world changing colour
because I say so.
Be ready to jump now, little things,
        jump for your own lives.
For I am letting go and leaving
slowly.

Potato Cuts

Now girls,
You are taking impressions
And transferring them to paper
Like a mental version of
A half potato dipped in poster colour,
Your neat design gouged out – so –
By a blunt knife.

We encourage you
To make impressions
Only be sure you do it properly –
Tidy potatoes, without smudges
Or fingerprints,
Not using too much paint.
Impressions
Should be contained.
We keep no gold stars
For messy workers.

See that you give a good impression girls –
Look, do as I do,
And don't spill
Anything.

 THELMA GOOD

Willing the storm
in over my head

Moved at a distance, I lie in wait
counting from the light.
One, breathe, two, breathe.

Not close enough, I lie in wait again
willing it above, not just once
but many times.

I want it.
Now over my head
again and again
stripping my senses
ripping everything
but the moment
away.

I will it.
All of it.
Light whipping night away.
Sound striking silence out.
The tingle as it hits,
the octarine afterlight
ozone in the air
elation in me.
Now.
Now.
Over me.

Rough Tor

I like to live near the edge
but you live on a knife blade
perched out on the tip point.

You took me to your special place
to Rough Tor, so I could see.
You walked out on a stone
sculpted free from the rest
by scour wind and snap ice.

Sure of your footing
you stood at the edge
the drop before you
the wind blowing
up against you
like a lover.

And I could only crawl
out just a little way
on that freed rock.

I could still see the land below us
but the wind's soaring caresses
I could not, can not ever share.

Version 1:
No More Bricks in the Wall

written just after the Berlin Wall was torn down by the people

The maps flew
their tent wings
crackled in the air.

The map makers
stood below
watching the colours change.

The maps swooped and soared
their patterns
some never seen before.

The hour was late.
The map makers set their nets
and enticing corn.

They turned the light low
and locked the map room.
Twice inside, once outside.
Then the map makers left
one by one.

Late in the night
the flutters in the map room ceased.

In the morning the map makers returned
quills and fresh vellum under their arms
their legal cats, one each, walked with them
on short leads.

The locks sprung back, the door opened
the maps tried to fly upwards
ensnaring themselves on the nets.

The map makers bent over the cats
and loosed them. The maps tried but the cats jumped.

The scrunch of cats' jaws on map wings
accompanied the squeaks of quills on vellum
as the map makers inked in the old outlines.

Later as the cats slept, replete for the moment
the map makers chained them up again.

Outside the monsters of the Dark waited.

Version 8: 1920-1990
Getting to the Roots Again

July 1990

I have heard of my fellows
stretched beyond the limits
and stuck to wires
on the outside.

I am inside still
and still inside.

The Director shifts his feet
in the long pile, deep
in the weave of his thoughts.

Every day he comes
stands before me,
runs a finger
round my edges.
My internal lines
fascinate him.

Each morning
as he observes me
he names my regions
stroking each name with his index.
It has become a litany,
a shortening litany.
To the west I no longer sense my extremities
and deep in the heart of me rhythms are recalled.
His litany seems to be calling them to their senses.
But still I am inside
but inside it is only I who am silent.

Under my fading inks
deep in the canvas
I feel the tug and pull
of those he names,
those the map makers had written
and some they left out, ignored, forgot.
The Director is remembering them
he traces even their outlines.

I see their names tremble on his lips.

How much longer   can   I   be   still?

To you all, afterwards

Let me imagine afterwards
when you, Giles, will be full
of langoustines and Armagnac.

And James with the one
glass I will leave you
brimmed with wine.

I see you Angela
deep in the feather-bed
I am lying on,

with Julian or some other
by your side.

Rory will be examining
for the umpteenth time
the Chinese vase
with the almost indiscernible
crack

and Alice with my best hat.

Confessions of a Spiderwoman

What a life!
Flies for lunch and flies for dinner
and the current mate for the morning after.
It's inconsiderate indeed to eat a mate after he's come
and before he's time to go but I need some fun
some spice in my life, and after all you know,
it's the one you have after gives you that glow.
You see I get this overpowering urge.
I've tried to give up. I went on a purge.
But it's built into us, in our species spec., you see
like the webs, the spinnerets and the eight knees.
There are advantages I know, I am sure
the consequences keep most of our emotions quite pure.
We're into celibacy and masturbation;
Papal sanction for one, the other relieves frustration.
But I just can't resist the small mate
every now and again I try out for a date.
I wiggle my eight hips, roll my multiple eyes
and oops, another mate is in for a surprise.
I just can't resist the nature of me,
to eat flies and mates, it's the making of me.

The inland train journey

We sat, our cases and bags, blocking the corridor.
Palms were read, fidelities discussed, and apples shared.
"I must show you what I've bought."
With a boy's self-absorbed grin,
from a plastic bag you pull out
a tin bucket, painted boats upon its side,
from a childhood forty years ago.
Our legs swing against the moquette seats.
We all have sand between our toes,
noses sun-burnt red, sea-smelling hair
our thin summer clothes, crushed, sweaty
damp from sand castles and rock pools.
Dirndls for us girls, and you in shorts,
the crab still moving in your back pocket.

 JENNIE HOUSE

On the other side of the river

On the other side of the river
the willows
familiar as trunk
and branch and canopy
smelling of earth and water
and distilling the light
into a trickery of flicker
draw back;
a mesmeric curtain
constantly billowing;
a pulsating, tendrilled flow
of spirals,
out of which
as if shaken from this
green river cloth
dozens of little brown birds
drop
and instantly rebound.

On my kitchen table

On my kitchen table
is a pot of blue hyacinths
cradled in moss.
At their base
the opening bells
are copper blue;
a high bright blue
which shadows
to lilac
where their strong perfume
oils them.
The perfume
eddies out from the flowers
in waves.

Once, I remember,
my very small son
his head no higher
than the top
of the table,
asked me
of a sudden –
what is death?

My hand
sifting flour or
peeling potatoes
hung suspended;
my mind was
a blank;
my eyes
re-focussed
on a bowl of blue hyacinths
And the words
that came,
said:

What oppression
it would be
if these full
waxy, scented
flowers

were never ever
to change
but to be
as they are
always.

Everytime
I come into the
kitchen now
I guard the flowers
with my affection
kiss and smell them
and touch them lightly
with my fingers

And as I take them
and as they give
themselves to me
something in them
changes

And now I see
they're dying;
and death is
in the air:

A friendly neighbour
young and merry
left in a car crash

The dog from next door
who made us laugh
has gone

And on the street
we speak
of war.

I wake in the night
very low
and it is dark

such is oppression:
little son
what have I done.

March · 7 · 1992

Today, at mid-afternoon
The old brown tea-pot –
not the small round one
but the large oval-shaped
filbert nut of a tea-pot –
fell and broke
into four
leaving its handle
in the hand
of the visitor
pouring tea for herself
and the three men.
I was in the back room
lighting the fire
and drinking up space
and felt the shock waves
rock around me as
I crouched before
the half-laid grate.
She wasn't hurt
I hasten to say –
and the others joked
about tea-pots
asking
to be broken;
but even as I
dealt out
the soothing sociable
rejoinders

I transfigure within
into the light
of another afternoon:

supple and strong
I have walked
beneath great
grey-mauve trees
and scrambled over
lichen-yellow rocks
beside the far calm
of a Northern loch.

Beyond the
dark massing
of the tumbling hill
appears a bright with
sunlight green grass
glen curving clear
down to the lapping
water's edge.
Beside me appear
a small boy of five or six
and a tall fair man
whose hair and jacket
camouflage
the dry colour
of last year's bracken.

A little way off
stands a house
neither too small
nor too big;
its slate roof
like an old jaw, agape
whistles the sky
and sheep and horses
have scattered and heaped
their fertile dung
about the front door-step.
The kitchen waits

in stillness;
a good-sized room,
bare save for
one chair and a table,
an empty whisky
bottle
and gleaming faintly
from the grey dust
of the forsaken
mantle-shelf
I reflect back
at myself
from the belly of
an old brown tea-pot
not squat and round
but surprisingly
oval-shaped
like a ripe filbert nut.

Old allotments

Slanting through
the gap in the fence
barbed with privet
we re-enter the secret place
just above the river.

Allotments once
before we found them
chest-high with heavy flowered
electric nettles
large with leaf;

lest we take the path for granted
that inches us
hands-up surrendered
to the tile-edged
stepped descent
of the space
of separate grasses.

Red-stalked
green-speared
pollen-headed platoon
islanding
the lemon-flowered
remnant cabbage.

Four garden huts
guard the perimeter
two to the right
and two to the left
the last of which
is the home on the range
the kernel of the nut.

And we sit there
in the sun
beside the shade
of the blue geranium
and eat our rations
from their brown
paper-bags.

From the briar
that snakes across the roof
into the lilac bushes
hangs a dark red rose
full-blown
above the water-butt.

The news tells us
of the approaching
invasion
of the yellow-clawed diggers.

Sunday alone afternoon

Sunday alone afternoon
Low grey cloud
Later turn to rain;
Quite cold. Autumn.

Bake cheese scones
to raise spirit
as baking powder
leavens the flour.

Clutching a warm
brown paper bag
with two from the oven
hurry out from the stippled stair.

Past the wash of coloured
crisp packets plastic bags
milk cartons and two presentable
boots at the door.

To the green patterning
of grass and paths and the trees
waiting damply
around the corner.

Up the slope, grass scattered
with fire twigs and branches
from yesterday's westerly wind;
turn into respectful shuttered drive –

in search of the nursing home
now housing old friend
(found by chance catching
sight of prints in art shop window).

Ring bell; ushered in to wait.
Suddenly she comes, surprised,
slighter than I remember
courage holding to the break

We talk. Her death is near
Her house of life untenable
Facts to face in the waiting
neutral space, two to a room.

All I say seems like cardboard;
flat mouthings of cheer –
meanwhile outside the window
a leaf lets go and the rain begins.

I tell of my next excursion
Evoking a jaunt for two
bearing the remaining warm scones –
but cannot bridge her desolation.

When leaving, my embrace
unintentionally rocks her
and I catch to steady before
walking out of the door.

Outside the rain is persistent.
I turn up my collar and hurry
back the way I have come.
I have an invitation to tea across town.

Half an hour later, curving
under the castle rock
the grass behind the black railings
thrusts wetly, intensely green

Tussocky, wildly alive
splaying fire earth works
singing out to me behind
the march of the iron dark rail.

PAULA JENNINGS

Feminist Poets

Some days I read your poems drowning,
clutching words in a thrashing sea
as your horizon lines up new meanings,
your waves transmute the savage sun
to spectrum colours I can hold,
your depths lead me up
through sediment, stripes of light,
turquoise air I burst through,
my fins flaunting their own sharp magnificence.

Some days I read your poetry in flames,
charred by the day's supply of casual hate
from eyes welded to the patriarchal view.
You show me fire that moves clairvoyant in the world,
visions so hot they take form and breathe.
Your words burn, witches stride from the page,
luminous,
and I remember who I am.

Invader

Through how many worlds
have you hurled yourself towards us,
rigid in that archetypal masculine shape,
torpedo,
missile,
your horizontal body helmeted,
programmed to find this time,
this target,
two women in a car, coming home from work.

Fuelled on beer, you roar through the dark
to the climax of your life;
scattering glass, you come between us.

All your lessons led you by the nose,
bull-like, to this curve of road,
to thunder under your own hooves
and stretch your shiny hide across the seats of a strange car.
No one taught you dying but you do it anyway,
while we, spitting glass, raining blood,
hold our connection,
hands clasped across your leather legs.

Assertively Trained

We will know them by the texture of their vocal cords,
toned but not bulging,
aerobicked in attractive leotards.

And we will know them by the modulation of their strides,
firm but not pushy,
in pretty, low-heeled pumps.

And we will know them by their gentle, ruthless needs,
manipulating nicely,
so as not to give offence.

And we will know them by the briskness of their hands
and tidy brooms,
cleaning up behind the throne.

But they will know us by our squawks and brashly gleaming beaks
as we dive,
impolitely accurate,
at the muscled heart of power.

Lucifer

To your left, just out of sight,
Lucifer falls and falls,
slender radiance in dark walls,
while you take the road in mapped sunshine,
slightly happy, slightly hollow.
Each day takes you closer to your hunger
as your wild ear slides behind birdsong
towards the bad bright angel.

Now the days turn and so do you,
a different path; inventing each step
as you edge into the feathered dark,
tracking a forbidden pride.

Coming Out

Afraid of their eyes,
I am afraid to tell.
Your eyes make me brave
and the coolness of
your breast unlocks my tongue,
coming and coming
out.

One Day

One day the words
will leap from me like flames
and I'll be a dragon,
ready to rout a whole flock of archangels.

One day these eyes
will unlock a monsoon
and the arks will fill with women,
and this heart,
calloused by its little wreath of thorns,
will put out buds.

Until then,
today is the spine-shaking drum,
today my heart cracks open like a nut,
today I step through without a guide.

Death Series

I

Two funerals in six months;
burning, burial.
My sisters are ash,
flesh sliding from bone –
how am I supposed to think about this?

II Helen's Funeral

Your coffin looks heavy.
You are big with anger, foaming blood.
Alcohol slaps against your ribs,
your chosen spirit, your guardian angel through this tangle of elements,
earth,
air,
fire,
water.
Firewater –
I hear it hissing on the altar, through the cheap wood,
as the priest, young and almost competent,
begins the prayers.

III Lucy Dying

Wanting only to stay in one place,
rooted and ordinary,
you are pulled on this harsh journey
through landscapes no traveller ever wanted,
and to such a destination.

You die slowly, your thin hands
torn slowly from this precious commonplace;
whispering through morphine instructions
that you hope will hold your world still,

keep everything the same:
the new blue carpet,
your small sons playing on the path by the magnolia.

IV After the Funerals

The months thump one on the other
and still death holds my ankles as I walk.
The pavement is too close
and too slow;
where did it get this power
to force such detail into single steps?
Its stony texture crowds my eyes like bees.

And all around me people swarm
in shifting patterns, smoothly,
as I falter in an empty place,
staggered by the busy desert of these streets
going on as normal.

V Dream

Love unearthed me,
cleaned the soil from my reluctant nostrils,
breathed in me.

I thought I was beyond sight
but her swift heart found me
aghast and unfolding.

VI Incantation

May the earth welcome them, these dear familiar forms,
may their deaths become part of life.
May they move whole in their fiercest visions,
may they gather all the brightness they have given,
may knowledge heal them.

 MARY McCANN

Working for Moloch
after reading Adrienne Rich

the cleaners are scrubbing the Institute lavatories
because women are supposed to do that

the girls are typing in the Institute offices
because women are dedicated and careful

the women are assembling printed circuits
because women are good at delicate work
and women's eyes are expendable

the young men are doing their PhD's
because young men are obedient and ambitious
and someone wants warheads
laser rangefinders
hunt and destroy capabilities
multichannel night seeking radar
and science is neutral

back home the wives of the PhD students are having babies
because women are maternal and loving
and who else can have children but women?

at the top of the tower the old men and the middle aged men
and sometimes one woman professor
meet to form plans, cadge funds and run the place
because obedient young men turn into obedient old men
and it's all for the good of the country
and defence funds are good for science
and science is neutral
and no one notices Moloch

the women bring them
clean toilets
cups of coffee
typescripts
micro circuits oh so neatly assembled
and children

and it's hard to see Moloch because he is both far away
                                          and everywhere
and they work on, priding themselves in their work
and no one asks to whom they are all obedient

and they say, "Who's Moloch?   Never heard of him"
as out in the dark Moloch belches
and grows redder and redder
and fatter and fatter
as he eats the children

Apples

a bad year for apples
they lie scattered like failure round the tree
marked by scab, bird, slug
and the brown that comes from the soil

a bad year for weather
wind, and driving rain
the tomatoes hang green behind glass

a bad year for your voice
they are crossing it out with X rays
day by day

a good year for potatoes
anything below ground does well
your Golden Wonders turning up
like muddy treasure

not a good year for old men, you say
the waiting room full of men who whisper
from all across Ayrshire
old headmasters, railwaymen,
anyone can get it
the lump in the throat

last night I dreamed
you had dug over the whole garden
brown soil spilling from the edge of the beds

under the failed apple tree
are heaps of shining Macintosh Reds
a harvest beyond dreams

quick, pick up your apples, I say
before the frost gets them

Tuna

in the supermarket
my hand, stretched out
for a can, stops

all round me,
creeping in,
rising,
filling the aisles
the deep deep freeze
the packed shelves
swirls the sea

and long silver fish, graceful
finely balanced, alive, marvellous
brush my sides

nerves brain eyes fins
a flow of life

holding my breath, possessed,
I lower myself to the water
let it carry me
I swim

far away, getting quieter,
the clank of iron, tin,
hiss of steam
swish of blades

the mountains of dead creatures
the neat tight cooked packed cans

Geese

Harperrig Bavelaw
Blackford Dunsapie

every September the wild geese

Barnacle Greylag
Pinkfoot Snowbird

embroider my local restricted sky

Greenland Spitsbergen
Lapland Siberia

every September the wild geese

Solway Loch Leven
Katrine Islay

I hear in September the beat of wings

On Craiglockhart Hill

on that hill
yes I think the trees were
witch's hair
and the wind, oh the wind was
crazy, a gale
and you laughed, I think, to see –
was it snow on the crests,
and a fire sky, and city lit like Christmas –
oh on that hill there was maybe
a new moon, but
it could have been blue
for all I knew –

for I looked at you

My friend Marain the artist

from a postcard of a painting by the same name
by Mary McGowan

my friend Marain the artist
sits in a field full of flowers

she is fat and golden
black hearts scatter her dress

green irises bend their sharp leaves to her
blue black iris flowers whisper in her ear

her black eyes look out intently
as her pen scribbles on the board on her knee

casually, easily, as natural
as mending a sock, or nursing a baby

her hand moves, sketches, pauses
her eyes look and look

she plants her feet in the flowers
sits astride

knees apart, like a grandma
she doesn't care who sees her knickers

the red of the flowers has got into her hair
it coils and springs round her head

her breasts bounce with the sweep of her arm

my friend Marain the artist
drawing the world

Museum

my niece is dancing round the museum
switching on steam engines and locomotives
beam engines and turbines
and the miniature huge pistons of extinct ships

child of the New World
five foot ten, fourteen years old and Canadian
she *just loves* the iron wheels
gears and shining cylinders
which rumble at her touch

the pride of tremendous bearded Victorian men
who kept their women at home in corsets

tall and pretty, in pastel sportswear and pink shorts
my niece dances from glass case to glass case
her finger gleefully hitting the red start button
first time, every time

neat, she says

Sky

remember it
it had no walls
no fences

you could fall upwards into it
you could ride a cloud ship
dizzy with distance

where it met the hills
you sensed a lovely crack to be explored
the horizon of every holiday

made you dizzy in your stomach, the horizon
and the zenith, all blue, made your eyes water

now the crazy satellites
are building barbed wire fences there
lasers, radio beams, electronic surveillance

building a roof where no roof should be
and it could fall in, any minute

and the children's innocent books still say:
sky, clouds, birds, blue, space

now they should say:
sky, danger, spying, death rays, hate

and the children ask: who does this?
and we say: men

and the children wonder why
men hate the sky

 RUTH McILROY

Bus-stops

As Japanese pause by a clear road
to let go past the unseen spirits
of broken cars, or check the mail-box
for letters never posted,
so we felt, that time,
the tremor of invisible connections,
a respect for what has not been.

From the train he pointed out a bus-stop
where once he waited at weekends
to return to house and wife
so long ago it might never have happened,
over the water, another age,
yet so vivid a time,
and the unseen net of memories and bus-stops,
journeys, loves and lives gone by
strung vibrant out from the carriage window
and settled quiet as spiders' silk
over the flat fields of Fife.

Later I reasoned that if we could only see far enough
the night would be ablaze, no sky between
with infinite stars' light.

The Coffin Lift,
Drumsheugh Nursing Home

Here is a concentration of death
coffin within coffin, like Chinese boxes
imagined in outline in this oblong
so the mind shuns, yet knows
exactly how they lay, and at which precise angle
their edges rim your knees like cool water.

Daily they were slotted in this space
and slowly fell; the confluence of years
carved out the figure of their passing
to give this place a serious core
in geometry which haunts me now
as lips of weirs and their glassy fall
slim stacks of city chimneys
runnels of water, transparent columnar things
making of this shape a quiet memento
as knee-deep in death I rise.

Annunciation

He appeared in the garden, to find her
in obedient blue among the white lilies
this is most unusual she said

Come inside and see my scarlet flowers
and took him into the kitchen
for want of anything better

And while they lay upon the kitchen table
she thought after all it is the best solution
he left with apologies for the awkwardness
sunlight came in through the open window.

Plenty

When I reached the bottom of the well
it was OK, lots to do
and all really new;
then they lowered a ladder
sent down a search party
but after a while they gave in;
now if I look up
one night in twenty
the moon says hiya,
how you doing, got lots to do?
and I say, plenty.

Interloper

All season I have been working in my garden;
after the winter came to an end
I dragged the rain-soaked branches from the lawn,
heaped them black and dank into a corner
where they dripped and ripened
then prepared the neglected earth,
digging the clay, from day to day
never so steady, so content

No-one disturbed me
and I didn't miss the company
till one day I looked up from my spade,
and there you were, balancing along the fence
in yellow shoes with a rose in your teeth
you are ridiculous

I don't care if you know a place with wild sweet peas
how could I leave my garden now
without the winter vegetables in;
please go away, and take those flowers with you,
I've seeds of my own in my back pocket
ready for the right season.

The other kind

Let me introduce you to my psychopath
who lives right here
where eggshell skull meets rigid neck
and everything is very clear

he sometimes puts his mouth to my ear
urgent, sexy, reasonable
dragging out my coward soul
like a ricketty cart over risky ground

that day I nearly fell, he unbalanced me
smiling like a wolf, beseeching
do it again, do it again
prove this is a world of grand escapes

not like the other kind, where people fall
and good is not rewarded, and parents die.

Acid

In the year I began to change
I saw my husband crossing a piece of grass
from a train, with a carrier-bag,
chin jutting against the wind. I wondered
where he was heading; for the bus stop
the flats, or what. First sighting this year.

At home I've cleared out everything
except the motorcycle battery; familiar, black
tidied away in the furthest corner
just daring me to.

All That

He made some big mistakes; he sold the sandwich bar
the year before the office blocks began to open.
The neighbourhood had been rezoned commercial; he must have
heard.

Back on the airport taxis, he'd invent life stories
until one day a passenger said 'We were in your cab last week'.
After that he grew a big fat stomach, putting it down to boredom.

The man's life was full of holes. Sweet basil grew along his
windowsill,
garlic from the Halal store, his table spread with onions,
plum tomatoes, parmagiana, olive oil from Lucca.

'You know what would pay round here' he said 'dog-walking.
'Walking people's dogs for money. But will he listen?
'Useless, that boy of ours, no fucking use at all'.

He knew he'd not got anywhere; he saw it in other people
and he could tell the difference; but didn't turn in and die.
People don't, they carry on, even when they know all that.

 SUSAN MAŤAŠOVSKÁ

"No maps can be obtained for this place"

Robin Morgan, Paranoia, from Going too far

In the crack between Sunday night and Monday morning,
Or on the outgoing eve of
The eighth day of the week
Or at the twenty-fifth hour that screams
I must seek my other hat
And put it on, firmly secured,
That I do not forget
Who I am
When I am not myself.
It is awful, this split place,
This edge or boundary;
There are no maps for it
No signposts.
Only blind necessity
Pushes me through the gate
To the other side.
I would have preferred to stay with you,
In the garden,
But the world outside would have it
Other.
They are not ready yet,
For us,
But a time will come
When we wait no longer.
The crack, the split
Will mend
And the map will have been drawn.

At home

Coming home was not easy:
I, the traveller,
Was long about avoiding it,
Seeking solace in dark woods,
Amid misty mountains,
Deserts where the sun sears down.
I let my flesh be mortified
By geography and tribal usage
Not knowing my own meaning.
But once, after rain,
My ear caught a sound in my innermost
And listening, I stepped, at last alone, to a doorway,
Opened, and looked through,
To a garden planted with honesty and lilies,
Where sang a bird in a bush
And I needs must listen
And enter at last.
It had been my point of departure
But I knew the place for the first time.

For there was a bird

For there was a bird, was a bird in a bush,
For she did sing both loud and insistent,
For she sang of Spring and renewing, which is come now,
For she was of the tribe of wren, or cave-dwellers,
For she was therefore strident and bright, in her singing,
For though I saw her not, I knew her nature and her name,
For I saw, in my mind's eye wind'seye window her dark beaded
                                                     twinkle,
For I saw also her ginger-brown feather-coat and her up-tip tail,
For I knew what she sang, and I heard it as one hears old
                                        knowledge,
For I heard it with love in my heart, leaping, as after rain when
                                                    sun comes
For I heard it as she worshipped and worshipped also.

On suffering a whole day at school before seeing my lover in the evening

It is 9.30, near enough,
And time is very long between the now
And the you.
There is a lot of noise in the signal
Between now and then.
It is largely, but not exclusively
Out of tune,
But I must suffer it gladly
For each of those that come to learn
Sees it as an event of singular importance
In their day, their week,
Whereas I, as a microcosm
Of same,
A chain of events, a series.
There are many violins between us, you and I
And a whole orchestra of miles and hours.
Oh, I would take to the hills, were I free of this all,
I would fly to you, singing,
And knowing you as I do,
We would meet on the other side
And you would catch me as I flew.

Witches

Witches have had a bad press
Of late,
Not to speak of previously;
But I see them everywhere
Not giving in,
Playing the system and winning.
I saw one
Park her broomstick on a double yellow line
And get away with it,
Another was pushing a cart round the supermarket,
Buying tinned pet food for her familiar
And a third
Embraced her lover on a park bench
Goes without saying
Behind a magic smoke-screen.
Witches are everywhere
They are.

The brown bird at Catterline

Walking down to the ache of the sea,
Down the brae,
To the sad and melodious stones on the beach,
When suddenly
A wren,
Tail-a-tip-top, ginger, twinkle-eyed,
Was on the fence
Speaking our language;
Sharp, up, do, she said,
Vanished in the undergrowth
And we walked on down
Knowing
That it was right to be, there,
To be,
To know
And to love
In that place
And all others.

Later, we talked,
We women,
Of women's things,
And learned
A new strength.
Back to the sea
We must,
Because it is.

The end of 1989

At the end of 1989,
The mist closed down on the house, bowl-like,
And we felt safe, unwatched,
Loving in this secret place
Where night never went
And day never came,
The sodium lamps outside
Telling perhaps of the end of time
That we had not noticed.
Later, a conspiracy of two in the supermarket,
I did wheelies with the trolley, exuberant,
Like a kid,
While you fought the cat food on the top shelf and won.
At the cheese counter
My intimate knowledge of your fridge
And our private jokes
Might have given us away
To one who could read the signs, the runes;
We felt secure enough, somehow.
Outside again, the mist hiding everything,
We kissed in the car
And went home
Having played at the dance
And kept silent, knowing.

What lesbians do in Jenners

The first thing,
Is to sample the perfume.
We tried *égoiste*
And liked its orangeness
(*Aqua Manda*
At six times the price),
Different on thee
And me.
Kiss in the lift
Between floors,
Hold hands in the coats department
Because the big yin's feart
Of the hole in the middle.

P.M.T.

(to be read through clenched teeth)

I have tits
(I mean, I always have,
But they HURT);
I can't park the car;
The force of gravity is very strong
And plates and glasses
Leap out of my hand
To their deaths;
I am cold,
Even when it isn't
And wear my nerves
All on my skin.
EVERYTHING is too loud
And out of tune.
Sometimes I write poems
Sometimes I don't,
But I almost always wash the kitchen floor.
The flood, when it comes,
Is a relief.

 AMY PORTER

The University

I think
  Those grey symmetric buildings
    Have organised the sky

  So that it sits in position,
    On top
  Like a painting.

I remember today

I remember today.
   The sun shone
         in a spangled stillness

      As a cracked window
         opened its mouth to the world
          Singing 'Cold Air'

I remember today,
   A man kissed a girl in the street.
   I walked by.
   Oblivious.

She will break with the first wave

Green water,
   In reflection,
      Shakes her face
      Makes it dance.

Look...
an uneasy lady
   with her own reflection
Poised
   On the thin edge of dreams......

She will break with the first wave.

Limits

The sea throws up white mysteries of foam,
Seen only by the stone eyes of the pier
Which it beats to blindness.

A man wrestles with the herring and the wind.

I feel the net of the frail mind
Stranded by limits
As close to the eye of stone and soil,
Wind and rain create
Their own rhythm.

Accident

A man
  A sail
    A boat
      White wave
        Deep water
          Silence.

Stones
  Smoothed
    Soothed
      by the sea
    Saw
      it coming.

'He caught his death', they said.

Each stone remembered as he lay silent.

The Funeral

A bird sings
A tattered harmony
Brittle in the mourning air.

Birch trees jut
  To the horizon

Their shadows
Etch pathways
On a snowlight
That tears eyes.

Twisted branches reach out
Accusingly to nowhere.

My foot snaps on a twig,
        Or was it
The fragile bone of some bird?

Delicate as your hand
On which my touch
Leaves no trace.

Scotland

Leaves gathered light on my window.
Beside one, a red dot like blood,
Marked out an inquisitive flower.

Behind, grey clouds hung in a stagnant sky,
Whilst obediently below,
Grey stone buildings stood symmetrically.

They made the flower look stupid.

A ridiculous red
    It stood,
        In gaudy gaiety,
            Exhibiting Itself!

'No good can come of that,' they said.

 MAUREEN SANGSTER

Aberdeen

No one can take
Aberdeen from me
that cold grey city

I only come
at Xmastime
when bleakness
seems a grand design –

chill air –
the seagulls rising
from the harbour
crying by the River Dee

This Xmas
a swooping seagull
dropped near me
its half-finished greed
I shuddered

at the exposed backbone
the sightless eyeball's sheen

Aberdeen
a cruel inset eye
a curious me

Scattering Ashes

I have
your ashes
flung out across your father's grave.
The North Sea pounded below, a deep fished sea.

The birds from the nearby sanctuary
made wheels in the air

and the glassless windows in the churchyard
gave long blue presents of the sea and sky.

Cold day for travelling yet we came. Away
from something dead and thin,

I found a solid poetry in that ruined church
and a conviction of where you returned to

through fire to dust to fire
for your silent nature was garrulous that day
your granite walls flung out sparks skywards –

where hands touched dust, the world was vivid –
specks of fiery ash whirling, merging, painting
all the pictures you didn't paint.

I ignored
my mother's troubled sadness
(the plastic container upset her)

I have
your ashes
warm pride against my cheek as fatherless I sleep
for who would have thought you had it in you

for such a homecoming? Buchan bound:
cliffs standing being eaten by the waves,
froth moving to the greedy plunge of gulls,
destruction and erosion saved by knowing
we return a soul singing in the bird's mouth.

I am Earth

I am Earth

where bulbs are pushed down under my soil,
where they will develop and finally appear,
sharp shoots, pale green in colour,
above my surface.

I am Earth

where roots extend, far below my surface.
These roots grip me, spreading out
their limbs, their fingers through me.
Hard to dig up and pull out, these roots
hold the trees and shrubs and flowers to me.
Through these roots, I feed
the leaves and apples on the tree,
the bright red berries on the shrub,
the pale white petals of Christmas roses.

I am Earth

I receive the dead in their coffins.
Spades have sliced through me
and made a deep space, temporarily, in me.
The words of a prayer hover over me,
the ropes rub against me
as the dead one comes in beside me.
"Dust to dust, ashes to ashes."
A handful of myself settles on the coffin lid.

The years pass. Decay, dissolution occurs
and the dead through me
are rerouted into these,
mauve crocuses streaked with white
opening up on a Spring morning
closing up as night falls.
These are my flowers.

I am Earth
the powerful strong snug dark place
home of decay and growth.

Woman

Men in the village are mutterin
mutterin, muttrin 'bout
the woman in the village.
Men in the village are judgin
judgin, judgin
the woman in the village –
she open
open to the touch
open to the touch of strangers.
Jealous bark of their anger
stokin
stokin to a crazy blazin
spit in the beer
beat with the fist
mad in the eye
bad bondin.
They'd rape her,
rape her, rape her
in their mind's dark clearin
for a woman like that
a woman like that
ain't got a wound for bleedin
ain't got a wound for bleedin.

I know her, I know her
I know this woman, she my sister.
Yes, she open
open to the touch
but open to the touch of livin.
Beautiful? yes
but her beauty
she know how to leave it.
Kindly? yes
and her kindness
she feed it,

this woman, my sister,
my sister, my sister
an' at the dance,
at the festival
she give to the spirit
not to the priest,
she dance with the dance
not with the chief
this woman, my sister,
my sister, my sister
is packin it in, she
learnin! leavin
the paths in the village,
going in her own direction
open to the touch of fun
open to the touch of sun
open to a world to come.

The men in the village
can't make her.
The men in the village can't take her
so they take her, rape her
in the dark outside the village.
Hard lesson in bleedin
hard lesson in bleedin.

Oh I'm sore 'bout my sister.
I'm sore 'bout my sister
her breakin, her bleedin
which men in the dark ain't seein.
I'm cryin for my sister,
I'm cryin for a world that's twisted,
I'm cryin by the grave of the future
if it's only hate that's breedin.
Is it only hate that's breedin?

Unpalatable

While a chicken
is eaten for dinner,
a lion is viewed
in the zoo.
Though a lion could
swallow its keeper,
lions in zoos are
subdued.

If a chicken was
but a bit bigger,
recognized as having
a roar,
we'd insist on
a zoo cage to fit her
when she beat on
her battery box door.

It all began with –
THE LIVER –
slippery and
rather red too
and now I've a
problem with chickens
and a sense of
injustice too.

Why don't we
eat lions in Britain?
I know
there are only a few.
But it would be
a gesture to chickens
from lions
who die in our zoos.

Out with Owen

Could you leave
your bag here
the attendant shouted
on Owen

Owen
while we
and a family of four
(all of us with bags)
climbed the art gallery's stairs
freely

Could you leave
your bag here
you young person
you black leather jacketed
young person
you person with
white paint painted onto
that black leather jacket

Could you leave
your bag here
the attendant said
and Owen descended the stairs
to do so

and did so
and the world was made good
in the eyes of the attendant

while the bombs beneath
our bulky coats
were only a handbag away

CHRIS SMART

Consumed

How would you like to go shopping,
pick up the groceries for the week,
at Fairway or Safeway,
some place that sells cooked chickens,
you know the kind,
turning round on a spit,
sizzling to a golden brown?
Just smell the roasted flesh.

Your husband and daughter
meet you
halfway down one aisle,
take the wrapped chicken from your cart,
eat it, wings and all,
fat running off their chins,
skin sticking to their fingers,
scraps of bones thrown back in your cart.
They open boxes of crackers and cereal,
ripping off prices and labels;
dip their fingers into the ice cream,
slip the cheese out of its wrapper
and break it into chunks, slap
it between slabs of whole wheat bread.

When you wheel up to the cashier,
they walk out the door empty-handed.
You pay cash for their bones.

Ode to a Clothespin

My daughter hands me the pins one by one.
Small wedges of plain wood,
identical twins, notched and grooved.
Sprung together like siamese twins;
the umbilicus, a tough coil of wire.

I pinch open mouth after mouth,
clip each sock and pillow slip
separately. I am generous.
The days of scrimping pins, doubling
diapers with towels, behind me.

The sheets buffet in the wind,
absorb sun like flags.
The pins
keep order   keep the peace
as they travel down the line.

My daughter plays with the leftover pins,
the red and yellow plastic ones
in the bottom of the ice cream bucket.
She clips one to the next, builds
a snaking train across the porch,
the last red one, a caboose
she will ride tonight
as she slips between
sun-filled sheets
and buries her face in fresh air.

Marks in the dirt

John the Turk sat beside
me, on a plank bench
behind his shack.

He marked the dirt
with the end of his cane,
over and over

circles
        arrows
crosses.

I don't remember what he said
only what he did.

He cut a plug
in a watermelon
to check for ripeness,
passed it over
on the tip of a small
black knife.

I remember the stench
of stale piss
by his shack,
garlic on his breath.

I don't remember what he said
only what he did.

Father

I hear what you say but I don't listen.
I never listen.
You talk and talk, obsessed
with the sound of your voice.
As a child, I listened to you.
I try listening now.
In a chair opposite you,
furthest from the fire, I hear you
say something, but
I don't listen.

I listen to the garden
standing in a circle of trees,
listening to wind in the pines
resonating silence.
I listen.

A tree trunk sways at my spine.
Night shelters and caresses.

Your voice breaks in.
Words, words, words.

On a Broad Reach

It's that twenty-eight foot classic
wooden sailboat, with a forty-foot mast
and sail area the size of a parking lot.
The one with the saucy stern.

She knocks down easy in a big wind.

He salvaged her from the bone-yard,
from a life propped up on oil barrels;
scraping, sanding and varnishing,
he rebuilt her,
put in a new engine;
launched her on the summer solstice.

She's got a mind of her own.

Inside, calm...
I watch the play
of light on gleaming mahogany,
then the sunrise through a postcard
window. He sleeps
with his back curled
against the ribs of her hull.

You must wear a life jacket at sea.

It has nothing to do with waves
breaking over the bow,
nor the boat heaving in a swell.
No, nothing to do with heeling over,
saltspray soaking my hair and skin,
feeling wet and cold to the bone.

I am afraid of losing control.

I am hopeless with knots:
clove hitches, reef-knots, bowlines.
My fingers fumble,
lose fenders overboard.

It's like orgasm,
between a man and woman
and the sea.

It has nothing to do with westerlies
blowing up,
going to weather, beating
dead down wind,
nor running before the wind.

We run her up on a rock,
on a falling tide, a falling tide.

I have trouble reading the charts,
tide tables, knowing the currents,
tuning in the weather channel.

What if it blows up a gale?

Free the sheets, start the engine,
turn back.

Women's Work

An image of a woman
through her kitchen window:
she passes a dishtowel round the rim
of a bowl, as if circling
the neighbourhood, the island
into other kitchens, where women
ladle soup, stew or vegetables –
hot and steaming – into bowls.
Meals for their husbands, children
and friends; round the table conversations
about how the vegetables were gathered,
how one manages to make the food taste
just right, how another chops garlic
or mixes salad dressing from scratch.

I watch the woman lift the bowl
into a cupboard and place it
in a stack like other dishes
ready for another day of eating
across the island, across the country,
over the ocean to France
or places I've never seen
like China or Russia
where I imagine bowls worn thin,
the porcelain blue flowers
circling the rims
rubbed pale.

Impermanence

Tree trunks, legs of giants, clamber round the cabin,
A voice calls, *look up, look up*

I sign my name, next to yours, a pair of names
permanent on glass, indelible as handprints in fog

The forest sings, slash fires smoulder, blood and bones
buried, I'm held in the forest's palm, crying wind

Doubled up, paired, a couple
playing at love, matchsticks walking hand in hand

I hold you closest when you are gone
push you away when near

Brief reflection
on a winter garden

Curly kale turns introspective
green to purple,
its bite enhanced by cold.
Transformed as camellia
and protected from winter kill,
it will be praised in May,
Queen of the table.

Weary of wind and endless rain
spring cabbage grows impatient.
It would like to mutate as Romaine
leaf green, cut free at midsummer.

The leeks' flat green leaves
limp as spent tulips
dip to the earth, a slide
for raindrops and worms.

Parsnips thrust deep in black muck,
pale and white as hidden skin,
the ghosts of the garden
introverted and longing
for recognition.

Shovels, hoes and spades
lean in a locked shed, out of trouble;
hoses coil like silent snakes
dreaming of apples.

Tarragon, mint and oregano
sleep like the gardener,
the scent of lavender trailing
through images of a perfect pumpkin.

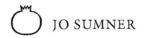 JO SUMNER

On Being Hollow

Hollow,
As a mighty cave stranded from
The encroaching sea,
No small embryo growing
In subterranean warmth.
A fat, flabby, starfish belly.

Hollow,
like a burst tennis ball
Game, set and void –
Understood now why some
Women quickly filled that
Yawning gap with more fruit.
Yet it sapped, forever sapped.

Never stated this hollowness before.
Just felt the space.

Snow Women

We built two, Zak and I,
As the full moon came
And the New Year
Diana was formed –
I wanted her to
Be a crinolined lady
But she became
An Ancient Deity with huge belly and breasts.
She stayed for a week
On top of the garden steps.
Next, we rolled a snowball
Around the garden
And Momma came to life.
Having no preconceived
Ideas this time
A squat Byzantine
Woman emerged
From the snow crystals.
I cannot explain why
Her face shone in the darkness
And I became so attached to her
Image that I was forever
Replacing the carrot nose,
Coal eyes and twig mouth.
As the Snow Queendom
Retreated.

Breast is Best

Breast is best,
Its worth is prominently displayed
In all ante-natal clinics.
Free flowing mothers' milk
Is natural nurturing.
But do it behind doors privately

Animals can do it anywhere,
Spring is a boob sucking symphony,
The suckling season.
Nipples nippling like mushrooms springing,
Young suckling, grabbing, caressing,
Gorging on breasts.

Full and fecund.

Aren't we meant to be animals
With sexual urges, copulation and Young
To keep our species going??

Are we meant to stop, block, deny
Our flow of milk,
And give our babies bottles
Sterilized, neutralized and accepted
In any restaurant,
Or on top of the Eiffel Tower.

Glorify killing.
Suckle in secret.

REBECCA WILSON

For Consuella

In silence we stand
Divided by the deep gorge that we
Cannot fathom:
The darkness of our differences.

You   strong in your conceptual cage
Where intellect and analysis
Are the only welcome visitors.
A place where you can be alone,
And more often than not,
You are.

I   weak in my hunger
For the opposite's flesh;
I lay, the hands of a man,
The weight of his body,
Giving me definition.

I am the container that leaks, bleeds.
You are the self-contained.

But I remember when silence fell
In around the words:
If I listened, I could hear
Your thoughts;
If you wanted, you could
Touch my mind.
A warm quiet when two
Women's souls met and smiled
In recognition.

Now we are speechless.
You, afraid of my weakness;
I, of your strength.
We see only red.

At this late hour,
fear of my weakness and my loss,
Rips muscles
Ribs part
Hard tears fall.
I reach in my strength,
Eyes blind,
Across the darkened
And ever widening gorge.

Turning point
– to my father –

I have been wearing your ghost for years.
Each morning I wrap your death around me
Like a second skin.
Dreaming, my hands are covered with blood,
Holding your shattered head,
Trying to sew you into one piece.
I never knew you in life;
In death, I've held you dearly.

But this little girl needs to grow,
To be watered by a fluid
Thinner and lighter than blood.
There is no longer room for two
In this body.
I need, now, for my bones to be my own.

Fear eats me in the night,
Slicing open my belly with his teeth,
Sucking on my heart, my breast, my mind's flesh,
Refusing me the separation of tissue from tissue.
The sky is ripped open;
It weeps and bleeds as we die
Together over and over again.

Under the light of sun,
I seek some way out:
Hungrily I finger small, hard pills
And sharp, shiny knives.
But in the warm bath, I hesitate:
If I open my veins,
Your fearful blood will flow into mine.
Your death will swallow me whole.

I enter a room with bare, white walls.
The paint peels and drops
Like tiny bits of dried skin.
I lie down, close my eyes.
I am shedding.

Gunshots echo again
But the sound is fading.
I can no longer feel your beard in my fingers.
Your laughter rises above my dreaming head
And floats its own way out the window.
Silence falls; the lights go out.
A new dream begins,
And I sing as I crawl out of your grave.

Dream of Bald Women:
A Letter to Mom

I dream of bald women

They have huge faces and eyes
That are sometimes blind.

Voices cry out:
"Shame, shame, you're just not right."

And so these women –
my women –
Walk in the world without hair

Marked
Their sin of not belonging now known.

Bald is ugly.

Bald is no sex
No place

Old and undesired
And now, shorn,
Without emotion or life.

I wake from this dream
Holding onto my bed
As you held onto yours
At your death
Four years ago.

Again
I've come back.
But this time
my eyes are different.

Your spine is bending over;
Shoulders curve to cover
Your shame –
Scabs that break and bleed
over breasts.
Fifty-seven year old breasts.

You've lost your flesh.
Shrunk.

Somedays I can see you getting smaller
As I stare and you disappear,
I become bigger –
Swelling with each inhalation I take:

Heavier:
A mass of muscle and fat and pumping blood
Awkwardly standing guard
As
You
Retreat
Into your bones.

If   I touch you
You will break;
Your arm will come off
In my hands.

Perversely you insist on cutting your hair short
So short that you seem bald
With only brown skin marking out
Where the hair used to grow.

You stare out your windows
But see nothing.

I don't see you:
You are far away.
Your soul so far inside.
So busy!

Your body sits still in the bed
Eyes move from ceiling to wall to floor
Unfocused
Working furiously
Taking apart your life
Putting the fragments in sequence
Counting up mistakes
Pushing, pushing for rest:

    "...not much time..going to have to see him again..
    good husband – but too strong... someways it's been..
    better since he died.... what shall I say to him?
           what have I done?
    had six children... three lived...worked..drafted
    blueprints...... I DID WORK, MOTHER...you can't say
    that I didn't make after... after I ran away............
    got to remember: tell Becky to tell my mother I AM FINE
    ...tell her not to come – don't need her, didn't need
    her then, don't need her now....need sleep..
    tired..so tired...
           got to get well.. go back to work...
    maybe I can silkscreen again...am I crazy?
    ....did try to kill myself once..lost – lost... my fault
    they shot him.. my fault the babies died... crazy
    a crazy woman...where is God?... never seen his face...
    where is Buddha?... need my breath..
           quickly – what have I DONE in my life?..."

I watch
And try to tie together the words that you say:

Last week you announced:

"Cancer is no disease –
It's my own anger and hatred and grief
Eating their way through my chest.
I am sending in the Blue Army
To meet the Red Cancer."

Yesterday you cried:

"You don't love me you don't love me.
Help me help me Becky.
Hold me.
You don't love me."

Today you lean over to me and whisper:

"Don't believe them.
I'm NOT dying
I'll get better –
It's just a recession.
You'll see...."

From your sleep you cry out:

"Oh oh oh"

Even your open mouth
I no longer know.
Strangely,
Only the shape of your feet
Stays the same.
I hold onto them – each one
Left and right
They're so cold!

Your jaw clenches and unclenches;
White teeth crush pain.

The Blue army won't work.
Finally
Exhausted, you sleep.

Waking
You cry out:

"Let me go –
I'm ready now –
Let me go

I want to die

Let me go

Goodbye... let me go...."

Go
Please GO.

The bald women are crying.
Their wet faces crumple
Eyes fall in
Skulls collapse

You die
They die.

I wake from this dream of your life.
For four years
I have watched and re-watched
Your death
Through my eyes.

Now
In my dream I have let you die
Your
Own
Death.

And I want to ask:

Did you make it?

Mom, do you have peace?

Are you there?
How do you feel?

I want to comfort you –
I want to say
Shhh!
Shhhhh!
It's o.k.,
It's o.k., Mom.

Pomegranate

Pomegranate began in Edinburgh in 1980 as a group where women writers could get together in each others' homes to share their work and offer constructive criticism and support.

Since then, Pomegranate have given many readings and performances, including those at Women Live festivals in the early 80s, and, more recently, at the Spring Fling, the Edinburgh Festival Fringe, the Traverse Theatre's 'New Writing' seasons and, with Women in Profile, during Glasgow's City of Culture year.

We have often been asked at readings if there is a group publication, but since a small booklet *Changing Rooms* in 1981, there hasn't been anything. This anthology brings together poetry (though we also write short stories, novels, plays and monologues) from past and present members, to celebrate Pomegranate's ongoing existence as a lively writing group, and to offer some of our work to a wider readership. We hope you enjoy it.

Pomegranate can be contacted c/o 24 Belmont Road, Juniper Green, Edinburgh EH14 5DY.

Biographical Notes

ELIZABETH BURNS has been a member of Pomegranate since 1990. A collection of her poetry, *Ophelia and other poems* was published by Polygon in 1991.

SUSAN STREETER CARPENTER grew up in Cleveland, Ohio. She was a social service administrator until she spent a year (1985-86) in Edinburgh and became a writer. She now lives in Yellow Springs, Ohio, where she teaches at Antioch College. She has a regular radio show with essays and interviews, and has just won an Ohio Arts Council Individual Artists Fellowship for fiction.

MAGGIE CHRISTIE writes as a radical feminist and born-again oboist. She lives in Edinburgh with her daughter. Her poems have been published in *Fresh Oceans* (Stramullion), *Whatever You Desire* (Oscars), *Original Prints 4* (Polygon) and *New Writing Scotland 10* (ASLS).

MARGARET ELPHINSTONE has published a collection of poems, *Outside Eden*, as well as two novels and a book of short stories. She is also the author of two gardening books, and has now left working as a gardener to teach English Studies at Strathclyde University. She has two grown-up daughters and lives in Edinburgh.

THELMA GOOD - born and brought up in Edinburgh, educated there and in Dundee. Now lives, and hopes to die, in Edinburgh. Does many things, few of them paid. Work published in *Graffiti*, *Fresh Oceans*, *Original Prints 3* and broadcast on *Morning Story* (BBC Radio 4).

JENNIE HOUSE was born and raised in Dorset. As a young adult came adventuring to Scotland which has become the base-line for home and work and further adventuring whenever possible.

PAULA JENNINGS lives in Fife. Her poetry has been published in *One Foot on the Mountain, Spinster, Fresh Oceans* and *Original Prints 4*. Her political/spiritual path is nurtured by lesbian feminism.

MARY McCANN lives in Edinburgh and is addicted to writing groups, including Pomegranate. Her work has appeared in anthologies including *Sleeping with Monsters*(Polygon), *New Writing Scotland 9*(ASLS), *Original Prints 4*(Polygon) and *The Crazy Jig* (Polygon).

RUTH McILROY lives in Edinburgh and works in the health service and as a Shiatsu practitioner.

SUSAN MATAŠOVSKÁ is a radical lesbian feminist, a musician (professional), astrologer (amateur), writer and gardener. She teaches the violin for her sins and lives with her daughter and two dogs and a cat.

AMY PORTER is a child psychologist who has taught Jungian psychology at the extra-mural departments of Glasgow and Edinburgh universities for a number of years. At present she has a social anthropology grant to work with Tibetan refugees in Nepal and North India and has just returned from sixteen months in Nepal, India and Tibet.

MAUREEN SANGSTER is from Aberdeen and presently lives in Kirkcaldy where she works part-time as an Adult Education tutor. Her poetry has been published in various magazines and anthologies.

CHRISTINE SMART is Canadian, a mother and a community nurse who lived in Edinburgh from 1978-83. Her poems have been published in *Northlight, Graffiti* and *Vintage '92* (Toronto). She is currently working on a Bachelor of Fine Arts in Creative Writing, and lives on Salt Spring Island, British Columbia.

JO SUMNER - Born in Staffordshire, living in the Highlands – has two sons, Simon and Zak - has taught, sung, written, wept - struggles to survive with positivism as a middle-aged woman.

REBECCA WILSON is a native Californian and Scripps graduate. She has seen the world through the eyes of a traveller, a waitress, a scholar, a stable-hand, a tutor and, most recently, as a journalist and fiction columnist. She lives and works in Northern California. She has published one book, *Sleeping with Monsters: Conversations with Scottish and Irish Women Poets*(Polygon 1990). Her poetry has appeared in several Scottish publications and her newspaper column 'Raising My Mother' appeared weekly from 1989-91 in *The Great Western Pacific Coastal Post*.